KINFOLK

JW SUMMERISLE

Published by Black Sunflowers Poetry Press
www.blacksunflowerspoetry.com

ISBN: 978-1-8382516-6-6

contents //

swithland wood

chestnut thicket and brush -

five broad leaves salt
breathing face headed
skywards, back.

microbeads of eyes all blue

the undersea (the
burning wood)

in hydrogen
and starving gas a glut
of dampened lung.

i pit; drymouth --

seeds of needle's dirt
froth lips, a
breathing horse of

twigs of needs.

a crying out for rain.

swithwood sea, please
take me.
conkers
charm in red and out -

i weep
for lady
jane and carry

      ten thousand in my mouth.

bradgate park

(i)

impossible replications of robins

crown the gap where
sense should be   logic

logically   a fly catcher king
of the old world   chest

flecked in blood

(ii)

brook of dragons / dragon brook

slate of shit and spring
of ice and spits in
fallow deer   white

tailing where it flows.

shallow   we

on the bones like
pearls and cave
teeth   catch

small things   (impossibly)

gilt bugs full of fire
find our guilty hands.

flushed and insensible dragons fly from water.

broken banks of footprints
fold back upon the
deer track   growling

 streams of ice.

seeming   we

uncover this under casing   winter bird.
robins sing   *poor me*   and shiver
dissolving

              deer into our foam.

scheduled ancient monument

chiffchaff the chaplaincy
insists that glass is liquid
and puts to sea secure
in garnets gushing salt
against our skin.

surely, sir, the brook is
shallow - both for us to
swim --   but

he insists

          black brick the
edges tinged. gold birds lead us
in. this holy place   please

hold us. diamonds flood
and barge. dirt loose cobbles
worrying coracles from our kin.

our skin. a
flesh boat, fresh
and pure. a chiffchaff
chiefly trapped. a
chapel pouring in.

bower close

(i)

the starving seem more fractious.

flesh more skin and teeth
pronounced more hunger. closely

wrapped and wrapped in cotton.

the whole hill – christo! fabric
wrapped and roped in wind.
ghostly.

it is an idol;

women wrap their wedding dresses
upon the rocks and beat them

screaming to be eaten.

(ii)

canal bridges teeth.
an abcess perhaps or
hotly worried halving pain
by patina. the victorians

crossed this way bent low;
crooked bridge by path.
she collared you

to say
all this
      is hers.

ashby road

the width of ashby road
bridges my wonder with birds
who scar the chestnuts with the
wounds of a wood green christ.

i mean, in my dreams the
pollards creep dead bodies from
the boughs and cut them down
to a dampness shaken from the sky.

as a child
i climbed the
low fence nighttime
headlights cars and carried.   i
hide in bushes and
bellies dived in deer

who doe you in the unmothered
black eyes back upon the road where

green spines spot the prickled
men who wait on bus and cry
red conkers – red the woodspot
pecker and his one unblinking eye.

i mean, my dream stigmata
larger than the stars jump starts

when autumn finds us high and hocking
great limbs from the grey god and his
bitter autumn sky. i dream the woodflesh

pink and weeping, star-leaves falling down.

i see the old men

absent bench and wreaths of metro
meeting by the way. they feast on
chestnuts, chest-struck birds impaled
and feather empty trees. i see
our bird plucked bodies wrecked
and naked in the breeze.

i dream a wider sun of ashby.
a ring of deer and dark. i see
the pollarded boughs above
where buses ought to park.

jane

i want to scream it until
each of my teeth has fallen
out. blood stick mouth pricked
hollow by hoping bones that
i can heave under the sheer
weight of my words.

my breathing mouth pearls sweat
and drip damping body red
like horses hauling the

ten thousand things   i

condense in calling
jane   jane   into

the sea that isn't.   the

ducks sink leaden
into pond and stink.

the woman comes
to warn me again.

argents mead

gloriana gilds leaves with browning,
folding yellow into furrows of the stars.

she is queen   or may be

brown thing with tiny hands and
foundling, furred in fawns and
local. hairs braided bony rocks,
small pebbles. broken glass. she's

skittish   scared to

ask us   almost

to bend the knee to break
the moat where nettles
choke the water into rings.

perfect. it is dirty. and she
is scared and small. she wants
us to lift the masonry and
build her castle walls.

memorial

this isnt tao. she pulls my mother out.

the real one. the one with brittle
hair that knots into the spiders
that occupy the hollows of the
deer as they display their
emptiness out on the priesthills
road. she's not alone.

there's the queen, of course,
who isn't the queen but really

a sort of self stuffed with sparrows
bled red to look like robins.

she speaks in parables which
only makes it worse. my
mother pulls her hair out
and puffs to suffocation on
poor cigarettes pinched
in her long yellow claws.

this clearly isn't tao. this is

the priesthills road run from
town pulled down in a
felling of deer. doe kill;

a dry mouth spitting split shells
of conkers crying out, just out.
just out.

angels

ford the trent. we are

full. sugar streaming from
the water frantic as
a flock of geese lifting,

clouding the sky with wings.

the contradiction

lincoln cathedral lights catch
our half cut heads. our

shirts miraculously white.

our voices unaffected by
the violence. magic

untainted by the iron.
i am honest in this

moment. honoured by the
blade and saintly. totally

unharmed. i cannot
be sad about this;

seeing the city lights pale
beside the flying buttress.

flights of hair
wrap me up.

nestled. cradled.
covered in a white cloth sheet

like a bier or a bride.
something perhaps better

than my head of bitterness.
beatitude and the ten thousand

things hanging from the
hard cut stones. holding

fast the spires where
angels would sit if only

if only if

there is no home

starvation headache. hold the crown.

hunger holds the gown in garnets.
gloriana hurts. she's

plain jane purple in the
tree of bruise fruits. her

damson flesh softened
to the stone.

brocaded beads of pearls
all green. sour taste.

curling tongue.
teeth all pronged in

velvet. vain girl.
she's starving

to be seen. nine
days is long enough

to be choked
upon the breath.

nothing but air
but brittle hair

and the heavy
weight of crown.

this bruising
weight of fruit

for care. we
cannot give her

this. gold spun.
her nose is seeping.

the flow of soar
and stern. how

strong in stupid
girl is given.

nine is nine
days long.

home

fascinated by the idea of elsewhere the

A46 opens trees up to a
kind of bareness that warms

weaving heat from the hardshoulder
that is lightweight and

almost beautiful   i

am not sure that you
know what prayers are
that you recognise distinct
letters from the mop
of dark that whets us
yet

the land holds out towers
to you   tolling

bells and you

ask me fancifully
about all of the other
elsewheres and ask
for their ringing

for their dark hides and
tar of morality   oval

roads singing us in
past the sapcote road
with suggesting that
i know the whereabouts
of god

dead man's bible

(i)

lilleys yard bones
and the broken deer
skull bind us

like a spell through
which the faerie queen
comes to visit

dipped in a gown
of blood like

she knows being
female starves

black eyes to
the whites of this

dust the

unswept cobbles
by the slums

where we walk
in the hope

of catching leaves

masons of the mother church
maximise their depth / obscured
in ringing volumes here
strays a wasted game i
cannot begin to play

genes for darker hair track drunks
amongst the headstones hammering
homemade faerie doors / the vandal
smashed pumpkins plead

perhaps we left something here
among the leaves and lost shoes the
cider cans all clasped in light like
the gods who give us dead queens
mean to find us gold / our mothers

and theirs bristle / a fools errand
gathering stones by the oldstone church
thinking to make light work of working
hearts / halve this half heart humanely

in varnish or boiled / please

we drop copper coins in the collection
for candles we burn without a word

there is no catchechism for this
no common english prayer

(iii)

small cathedral organ
blocked in wood in
conkers shocked to
stillness shocked to
quiet servitude
                    it is
a wedding of the
headless blessed
by a thousand leaves

that brown after a fashion
and linger   hands
of gold pressed close

(iv)

leave behind this
motherless this
gutless peak
this witless
bird on its
travel east

i am forgetting
already how

to distinguish
wings from below
or how
calling
back to birds
makes them hazel
so

take this
for what it is

wet hand of
chestnuts coursing
cold without their culture

royal united hospital

damp spot of shells

swells the fur
edges the mouth &
pierces the skin

harebells pink and
purple lips flower

headless women
administer medicine
and it lulls us

to speak

like a queen
or a mother

maybe

Notes

Swithland Wood is an area of ancient woodland next to Bradgate Park in Leicestershire. Information on display at the Bradgate Park Visitor's Centre states that the 'S*withland'* was a place of burning.

Bradgate Park is an enclosed medieval deer park in Leicestershire and the former home of nine days queen, Lady Jane Grey.

The chapel of Bradgate House is the only fully surviving part. It has protected status as a *scheduled ancient monument*. It also has cobbled flooring and diamond latticed lead windows.

The Danehills of Leicester are said to be the home of child-eating witch, named Annis. According to folklore, she would hang the flayed skins of children outside her cave (often called her bower) which is now filled in and, part of somebody's back garden on '*bower close*'. The poem conflates the bower in Leicester and basin bridge in Hinckley. It also mentions the artist Christo who, with Jean-Claude, would often wrap landmarks in large white cloths.

Ashby Road is the main road into Hinckley. a cemetery occupies a long length of it on one side, with tall trees on the verge outside. Priesthills road, Lilley's Yard, Sapcote Road, and the A46 are all routes in, out, and through Hinckley.

Argents Mead is a green space in Hinckley, where there is a war memorial on top of the remains of a Norman motte and bailey (the only remnant of which is a large hill and half a moat which is now a duckpond), and an open field that backs onto the 900-year-old Saint Mary's church & graveyard. *dead man's bible* refers to the Saint Mary's Area, and also to the organ of Leicester Cathedral.

27

Black Sunflowers Poetry Press

Backed by an array of artists, activists, poets and poetry fans from all walks of life, Black Sunflowers, the UK's first crowdfunded poetry press, came into being in March 2020 with a pledge to publish and promote the work of women, older women and Black poets from the UK and around the world.

www.blacksunflowerspoetry.com

CPSIA information can be obtained
at www.ICGtesting.com
Printed in the USA
BVHW041829050822
643909BV00009B/553